Over the Edge

By Julia Green

illustrated by Priscilla Lamont

Contents

PEARSON

Longman

Text © Julia Green 2004
Series editors: Martin Coles and Christine Hall

PEARSON EDUCATION LIMITED
Edinburgh Gate
Harlow
Essex CM20 2JE
England

www.longman.co.uk

First published 2004

ISBN 0582 79641 5

Illustrated by Priscilla Lamont (Heather Richards)

Printed in Great Britain by Scotprint, Haddington

The publishers' policy is to use paper manufactured from sustainable forests.

Chapter One

Barney stood at the bus stop in his new school uniform. It was the first day of the new term at the new school.

"Don't worry!" Mum said. "Everything will be fine. You go to the main hall with all the other Year Sevens, remember? And just ask, if you get lost. Now, have you got your money? Bus pass? I'll meet the bus this afternoon, shall I? Walk back with you?"

"No. I'll see you at the house. Stop fussing," Barney said. He ducked away when she tried to kiss him goodbye.

From the top of the bus he watched her walking back down the lane. She looked small, suddenly. And a long way away.

In the mirror in the top front corner of the bus he watched other kids getting on at each stop. Green tops, black trousers. Some of them looked enormous. They thundered up the stairs, banged bags on the floor, shouted at each other. Barney slumped down in his seat, suddenly too conspicuous in his brand new clothes and too short haircut.

Behind him, someone laughed. "New kid!"

The bus chugged slowly up the hill towards the school. Barney could see it now: the tall buildings, rows of windows. His stomach churned. He couldn't remember where he was supposed to go. What had Mum said? He hadn't been listening. If only Dan and Mick were with him now. They'd be going to their new school together, with all the other kids from their old class. Everyone except him. It wasn't fair, moving house just when he was about to start secondary school.

The bus stopped. Feet thundered down the stairs. Someone's bag caught him in the shoulder. He felt sick. He waited till almost everyone had got off, then he joined the back of the long queue jostling up the drive and through the school doors.

The smell hit him. Polish. Dinners. Sweaty
bodies: that smell all schools have. He hesitated.

"Year Seven?" a smiling teacher asked him. It
must be so obvious: new boy. No friends. Weirdo.

Barney nodded.

"This way, then, into the hall." She held open a
door for him.

He couldn't run away now. He bit his lip, hard,
and walked slowly in to join the seething mass
of Year Seven kids. Row upon
row – hundreds of
them. Not a single
face he knew.

Chapter Two

"Sit down! Now!"

Where? Barney looked in despair round the science room for a space at a table. Everyone was sitting down except him now. Some kid turned round and laughed. "Plenty of space next to Carly!"

"Stop talking!"

Barney felt his insides curl up. Seemed like he was in trouble in the very first lesson before he'd even sat down.

"Sit! There!" A bony hand pressed him down into a seat at the table of girls next to him.

"What's your name?"

"Barney."

"Barney what? Stop mumbling!"

"Barney Eliot."

"Barney, Sir! You address me as 'Sir' when you speak. Got that?"

Barney bit down on his lip. This was worse than he'd ever imagined. "Yes, Sir," he managed to squeak. The whole class had gone silent, everyone watching him. He felt his face go red.

"He's horrible," the girl next to him whispered. "Everyone knows that. Lucky we only got him for half the science lessons. Don't take any notice."

Barney wanted to ask her how she knew that. But he didn't dare. The teacher was standing at the front now, taking the register.

Barney looked around. He was the only boy in the entire classroom sitting next to a girl. And there was something odd about this girl. Carly. Her uniform was much too big for her. Her hair stuck out like a messy bird's nest. She smiled too much. Typical. He'd ended up in the worst possible place in the whole room. Everyone would laugh at him.

The girl nudged him. Grinned.

"What?" he whispered.

"Barney Eliot? For the third time of asking?" The science teacher glared at him.

All confused, Barney stammered. "Yes. Present."

"Yes, Sir!"

A faint ripple of laughter went round the room.

What was the matter with him? He'd drifted off, not realised they'd got to his name in the register.

He tried really hard to concentrate for the next bit of the lesson.

"Not got off to a very good start, have you?" Carly said to him. Barney didn't answer. The girl next to Carly joined in. "One more thing and you'll get a detention. Three things, it is."

Shut up, he wanted to say. Shut up and leave me alone.

Now the teacher was handing round new exercise books.

"Okay, everybody. Listen. Copy this onto the front." He wrote his name on the board for them to copy, and the word, 'Science'.

Where was his pen? Barney fumbled in the new pencil case. For a horrible moment he thought he'd forgotten it, the brand new ink cartridge pen he'd got down town with Mum. But no, there it was.

The teacher stalked round the room, peering over people's shoulders, making comments. He seemed to stand behind Barney for ages.

Finally he spoke. "And what's that supposed to

say?" He pointed to where Barney had written the name.

"Mr Lawson, Sir," Barney whispered.

"But it doesn't, does it? It says 'Mr Lason'."

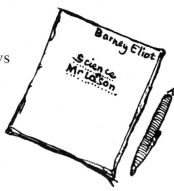

Barney tried to squeeze a 'w' between the 'a' and the 's'. It made a nasty blue blob.

He didn't follow much of the lesson after that.

"He's just picking on you," Carly said, too loud. "They do that to me, usually."

Barney kept his head down.

* * * * *

At break, he stood at the edge of the field and watched some older kids kicking a ball round. The rest of his tutor group seemed to have vanished. Beyond the football field was another, bigger space, with a running track marked out. For the next fifteen minutes, Barney imagined he was running round the track, and then, just as the bell went, he imagined what it would be like to just keep on running … out of the field and down the hill and on and on all the way home. Their old home, not the new one.

The corridors swarmed with people who all seemed bigger than him. You weren't supposed to run, or push, but loads of people did. Barney looked hopefully for someone his size who looked vaguely familiar and who might know where M7 was.

A small gang of boys holding their timetables like street maps in front of them were following a boy called Jamal with spiky black hair. Barney recognised him from the science lesson. Barney tagged on behind.

At lunchtime, it was so crowded in the hall that it didn't matter so much that he didn't have a friend. He queued to get his food, then took his tray to the nearest space at a table and ate without looking at anyone. The noise was so loud his ears began to hurt. There was still the whole afternoon to get through.

Because it was the first day, they had an extra long time in their tutor groups instead of the last lesson. Mr Parnell, the tutor, was funny, and told jokes, and didn't mind people talking. He gave them a little talk about getting organised, having the right equipment, homework. By the time he'd got onto the school anti-bullying policy, Barney had got a headache and felt very sleepy.

"All right, Barney? All a bit much, eh?"

Mr Parnell's voice interrupted Barney's dream. He had been about to win the junior marathon, only something was wrong with his legs and the racetrack had turned into a sort of river.

He stared, blinking, at his teacher. "Whazzat?"

"Time for your afternoon nap, eh?"

Jamal and Pete sniggered.

"Fill in your worksheet, and then swap with someone else."

Barney looked round, bewildered. Everyone was busy writing. He looked down at the worksheet. *Getting to Know Each Other*, it said at the top. There were questions to answer, and boxes to tick.

My favourite place is . . . The skateboard ramp in the park near where they used to live – in town – where he used to hang out with his mates Mick and Dan? His old room, in the flat? He didn't want to tell anyone about his favourite place. Next question.

Best sport?

That was easy. Running. He was the best in his year in the old school.

He'd spent too long thinking about his answers. When he looked round, there wasn't anyone left to go with.

"You'll have to join another pair," Mr Parnell said. "Team up with those boys behind you. Pete, is it? And Jamal? Move your chair round."

Barney saw them give each other a look. He sat miserably, half turned away, as they carried on talking about some computer game he didn't have.

Five minutes before the end of the day, Mr Parnell told them to pack up. "Well done, everybody! First day over. Tomorrow will be easier, now you know each other, and can find your way around. Off you go."

Easier? Tomorrow? The knot in Barney's stomach tightened.

Barney trailed out to the bus stop after everyone else. As each bus came, kids crammed on. He got a seat at the back of his bus, number 7, downstairs, and stared out of the window all the way. How would he recognise where to get off? What would happen if he missed the stop?

At each bus stop, people piled off, till there was hardly anyone left. At last he thought he

recognised the line of new houses. Then he
glimpsed the river through some trees and knew
they must be close. And there, at the roadside, a
small familiar figure, staring anxiously as the bus
got nearer: Mum!

Chapter Three

She greeted him as he stepped off. "Hello, love!
Thought I'd meet you, first day. I know you said
not to, but I happened to need a little walk!" She
grinned.

"Mum!" Barney squirmed as she hugged his
shoulders. But inside, he felt the knot unravel a
bit.

"How was it, then? Meet anyone nice? Expect
you're tired. Got any homework? What are the
dinners like?" She fired questions at him as they
walked down the lane that led eventually to the
Greenhill estate.

"All right," he grunted. He wished she'd stop
asking him stuff. He was so tired. His bag
dragged on his shoulders. He'd carried his stuff
around all day, PE kit and all, because he'd
forgotten to ask about getting a locker.

Inside, he slumped in front of the telly while

Mum made supper. Dad wouldn't be back for three days; he was driving the lorry through France and Germany. When Dad was away they usually ate their supper in the living room in front of the telly.

"Why don't you phone Dan, or Mick? Find out how they got on at their new school?"

Barney scowled at Mum. Didn't she know anything?

He heard her later, talking down the phone at someone. "Fine," she was saying. "Yes, he's a bit tired, I think. Well, that's to be expected. New house, new school, not knowing anyone yet. It's a lot to deal with all at once. And boys – well, you know. They don't tell you much, do they?"

She made him pack his bag ready for the next morning before he went to bed. He had to hang up his uniform ready. She set the alarm for 6.45.

"I won't be home from work tomorrow afternoon till late. So have a good school dinner, and get yourself a snack when you come in. Yes? You've got your key?"

Barney nodded. He listened as she went downstairs. He heard her switch the kettle on, and then she put on a CD.

Barney lay in the dark, his stomach churning over and over.

Then Barney started thinking about how many more days of school there would be after that. On and on. How many exactly? Five a week, fifty-two weeks in a year, at least five years, or seven if you stayed on (no way!), which made how many?

One thousand and three hundred, although there were the holidays, so more like ...

One thousand and fifty school days then. In his head, he crossed out the first one. The rest queued up in his head in a long line, like dominoes, or skittles in a huge bowling alley so big you couldn't see the other side.

Chapter Four

Since Mum wouldn't be there, it didn't matter if he was late home after school the next day. When he got off the bus, instead of taking the lane down to the estate, Barney went the other way, towards the river. He crossed the field. The grass was sopping wet. It flicked up his legs, leaving muddy splashes on his school trousers.

There it was! The river swirled, brown and muddy after all the rain, tugging at the banks. It whooshed and slurped, and then, further down, it smoothed itself out ready to tip over the edge of a weir.

In the shallow edges he could see small fish. He peered over the edge of the bank. The water was scummy, stinking. Then he started to slip, and had to grab a tree branch to lever himself back from the water's edge.

Cool. He'd come back here. Get a fishing line,

even. And some time, he'd try and cross over that weir, balance along the edge to the opposite bank.

He found a way back to the estate along the river, scrambling through a hedge, and then through a gap in a wire mesh fence. He got a bit lost once he'd crossed the big field into the estate because so many of the houses looked the same. They were still building the ones nearest the river.

Some little kids were riding bikes around a small front garden. They stopped and watched him. A bit further on, a boy of about eight or nine watched Barney through an open upstairs window. So there were other kids on the estate. He hadn't seen any before. It wasn't like their old street in the town, where everyone played out together after school.

5, The Beeches. It just didn't sound right. There wasn't a beech tree in sight, in any case. Barney put his key in the shiny new Yale lock, and banged the front door too hard back against the wall as he went into the hall. It left a dent in the newly painted plaster.

He kicked off his muddy shoes and went into the kitchen. There was a note propped up on the table.

Pasties in the fridge. Warm one up if you're hungry. Hope you had a good day at school. See you 7-ish. Love Mum

Barney filled a bowl up with cereal and spooned golden syrup on top, then milk. He took it into the front room and sprawled on the floor in front of the telly. Then the phone went. He picked it up.

"Hi, it's Mick. Want to come over?"

"Can't. No one's here for a lift. What're you doing?"

"Nothing much. You?"

"Nothing."

"What's your new house like?"

"Boring."

"School?"

"Big. Yours?"

"Okay. Get your mum to drive you over on Saturday?"

"Okay. I'll ask."

"See you!"

The house seemed even quieter after he'd put the phone down. Barney watched a programme about the duck-billed platypus.

Then he remembered he had homework to do. He got his planner out and read what it said.

English: Start writing your autobiography.
For next lesson.

He'd copied it off the board at the end of the English lesson, but now he couldn't remember what an autobiography was. Something like a story? He put the book away again.

Then he wandered into the kitchen, ate his pasty straight out of the fridge and drank the rest of the milk.

Finally he heard the car. The clock said ten past seven.

At bedtime he remembered about the homework.

He went back downstairs to check his timetable, to find out when the next English lesson was. Second lesson tomorrow.

Mum called out from the kitchen. "Have you got your bag ready for the morning?"

Quietly, Barney took out the day's books and packed ready for the next.

"Yes," he said.

"Good. Now get back to bed."

He hovered in the doorway. She was writing something.

"What are you doing?" he asked her.

She looked up at him and smiled. "Choosing things for the new garden. Anything you'd like?"

"A tree that will grow really huge, for climbing," he said as he went back upstairs.

The orange glow from the street light filtered through the curtains. His school uniform, hanging on the side of the cupboard, cast a shadow over the bedroom.

One thousand and forty-eight more days, he thought just before he drifted off to sleep. And then he remembered about the river. Perhaps if Mick and Dan came over ...

Chapter Five

"Look at you! What have you been doing? Look at the state of those trousers! You can't go to school looking like that! And you haven't got another pair. What were you doing?"

Barney mumbled into his breakfast. "Sorry."

"Did someone push you over? Was that it? Is someone bullying you?" Her face went all worried-looking.

"No. Calm down, Mum. I just went across the field, that's all."

"Well sort yourself out. Hurry up, or you'll miss that bus. I'll be home early this afternoon. And Dad's back later today."

Barney escaped before she could see the state of his shoes.

On the bus, he thought about the English lesson. What could he say? He'd forgotten to bring his homework in? He'd done it on the computer, and then it wouldn't print off?

"What's yer name?"

Barney looked up. Someone was talking to him. An older boy, tall and stringy, with a thin face and short fair hair.

"Me?" Barney's voice came out a bit squeaky. "Barney," he muttered.

The boy announced it to the entire bus. "This is Barney. Barmy, right? Or born in a barn, perhaps?"

Two girls tittered.

Barney stared at his own feet.

"Barmy Barney's a bit shy, aren't you? Aren't you?" the boy said, even more loudly.

Barney couldn't think what to do. His neck had gone prickly and that meant it had gone bright red, like his cheeks.

"Shut up, David Blake! Leave him alone," one of the girls said.

"He's sweet," the other one said.

Barney's ears were burning now. He stared, hard, out of the window, willing the journey to be over.

When the bus finally stopped outside school, David Blake trod on Barney's foot as he went past. Barney winced.

"Ooh, sorry Barmy! Did that hurt?"

The girl behind David smiled a fake sort of smile at Barney. "Have a nice day!" she said in a pretend American accent.

It was as if she'd cast a nasty spell on the day. First there was maths, and they had a test, and he suddenly found he couldn't remember any of his seven or eight times tables. Then there was English.

Miss Farley smiled brightly at the class. "Our project this first half term, as you know, is 'Autobiography'. The story of your life. Let's hear some of your beginnings," she went on.

Neesha read hers first, then Jody. Eventually, Miss Farley started to pick on people from the back of the class. Moses had written something really funny and everyone laughed.

Carl's was sad, and Miss Farley got a bit

flustered because Carl didn't know anything about his real mum and dad, and talked instead about all his different foster parents. Then she looked at Barney.

"And now yours, Barney?"

His lips were dry, his hands sweating, heart thumped. The knot that seemed to live permanently in his stomach now turned into something alive, like an eel.

"I think I'm going to be sick –"

"Quick! Let him through!" Miss Farley shouted, as Barney made a dash for the door.

Down the corridor, left, right – he wasn't sure how, but a sort of instinct led him to the boys' toilets and he got to the cubicle just in time.

Someone knocked on the door. "You throwing up?"

Barney crouched, shivering, his mouth full of the sour taste of vomit. He couldn't speak.

The voice came again. "I'll get a teacher."

Barney heard footsteps, a door banged. Then it was silent. He flushed the toilet, put the lid down and sat on it, head in his hands. His

head ached. He felt like crying. He wanted home.

He heard more footsteps, a teacher's voice he didn't recognise: "All right, lad? Unlock the door when you're ready and we'll take you to the medical room."

Barney came out, washed his hands and his mouth at the basin. The teacher steered him along the corridor past the ladies at the Reception desk to a little room with a couch and a chair and one window.

"Have we got a number to call someone at work? At home?"

Barney nodded. "Mum. Work."

Barney listened to the footsteps going away again. The corridors echoed, a gloomy sound. He looked out of the window. Then he closed his eyes to wait for Mum. He didn't feel sick any more.

It seemed ages. He heard the bell go for next lesson, the school pounding with noise, and then silence again. Finally, the door opened.

"Hello, son."

It was Dad!

"Get your stuff, then, and we'll get you home. Mum's cooking, eh?" Dad laughed.

Dad chatted about his long-distance trip as he drove Barney home in the lorry. Barney loved the lorry usually. You felt so high up, you could see everything for miles. They usually mucked about together, making up stuff about the other drivers.

"Straight to bed when we get home," Dad said, his face dead pan.

"What? No way! I was just sick!" Barney started to argue.

Dad looked sideways and grinned. "Me, I mean. Not you. Been on the road for nearly twelve hours and I need a kip. What's it like then, the new school? You getting on okay? You make sure you make the best of this opportunity. I never did and look at me. You want to get a few qualifications under your belt ..."

Barney felt miserable again just thinking about it. "I don't know anyone," he started to say, but Dad was tuning in the radio and not really listening any more. Dad started singing along.

The house was different when Dad was there. Noisier, more fun. Dad turned the radio up loud and sang along even if he didn't know the words. He could sit in a chair and be asleep within two minutes, whatever time of day. He said it was an art. "Power naps. It's the latest thing in smart offices," he liked to tell Barney.

While Dad slept, Barney lay on his own bed, staring out of the window, thinking about the English lesson. He got his exercise book out and a pen, but then he couldn't think what to say, because he kept imagining having to read it out in front of the class. They'd make fun of him. Or yawn, bored. Or roll their eyes. He wished he could make them laugh, like Moses. That was the way to get people to like you, to be friends. Only how? What was funny about being born? He couldn't remember any funny stories about himself when he was little.

So he gave up, and changed into ordinary clothes, and went out, down to the river. He took his penknife so he could cut sticks.

The water was rushing along, almost up to the top of the banks. It swept stuff along with it: dead branches, bottles, cans, plastic bags. He poked with his stick at the junk caught up in the reeds near the bank. A huge tree branch and a rusting supermarket trolley had become trapped at the weir, but much too far out for him to reach.

He peered at the brown water. You wouldn't want to

fall in. Further up, near the bridge, there was a sign warning 'NO SWIMMING', with a picture of a person with their arms up, half covered in wavy lines. Who on earth would think of swimming in that?

* * * * *

When he got back, Dad was frying up eggs and bacon and the house was warmer and more homely than it had seemed for ages; more like the old flat. They ate together, and Barney told Dad about the river.

"You be careful, though," Dad said. "Water's dangerous. Especially when the river's in flood. Even for a good swimmer like you."

He took a big bite of toast. "Show us your school books, then."

Barney got them out and spread them on the table. Dad moved the ketchup and vinegar out of the way. "Keep 'em clean."

"I've got to write an autobiography," Barney said. "What shall I put?"

Dad thought for a bit. "You could say it like you were there – well you were, of course, but like the baby – you – knows what's going on."

They had a go together. It was easier with two of them.

First thing I saw was this weird *bloke* with cropped *black* hair and brown eyes and a huge grin on his face going all gooey over my tiny fingers and toes. That was my dad. He doesn't have much hair left now, and he doesn't go gooey, except over doughnuts or sometimes my mum, when he's just back from a long-distance trip in the lorry.

It took ages to write just that, and it still sounded stupid. He'd only got to the first minute of his life: how was he going to manage doing eleven whole years? By half term?

The eels in his stomach were beginning to squirm again. His hand ached.

"Don't hold that pen so tight," Dad said. "It's only a pen. It's not going to escape."

* * * * *

In the afternoon, Barney helped Dad clear some of the boxes in the garage.

"Look!" Barney pulled a handful of small Warhammer figures from the depths of a cardboard box. "I painted them well, didn't I?"

He and Mick and Dan used to have complicated battles on the carpet at Mick's house. Saturday mornings, they'd meet up at the model shop down town to buy more figures. It must be

worth a fortune, this whole box full. Barney
lugged it upstairs. He got the figures out and lined
them up on the floor in battle formation, but they
didn't seem exciting any more. And it made him
think about missing Mick and Dan. And then he
started thinking about school again. And felt sick.

Mum cooked chicken for supper in honour of
Dad being back, and luckily Barney had stopped
feeling sick by then. Dad washed up while Mum
helped Barney write some more in his English book.

"Early night for you," Mum finally said.

Another day done, Barney thought as he lay in
bed that night. One day, and then the next, and
then the next. Soon a week would be over. He'd
forgotten to ask Mum about Saturday, getting a
lift over to Mick's. He needed a bike. If he had a
bike, he could cycle there by himself.

Chapter Six

"Ouch!" Barney put his hands up to his ears.

This was the third time it had happened at school, now. This little kid had got it in for Barney. He kept coming up behind him and clapping his hands into Barney's ears so hard it made his whole head ache.

This time, Barney twisted round, caught the kid's wrist and dug his nails in.

"Help! He's hurting me. Get off you great bully!" the boy shrieked.

Everyone in the queue for science turned round to stare. Mr Lawson stalked along the line, glaring at everyone till he got to Barney.

"You again. Not learned your lesson, eh? See me at the end of class."

"But he started it," Barney tried to explain.

"Don't you dare answer back!" Mr Lawson thundered.

The boy smirked at Barney. Barney felt like thumping him. He would, when he got the chance.

The science lesson was quite interesting; Mr Lawson did a demonstration on expansion. He had a Bunsen burner and a steel rod with a bolt at the end, which he heated up. The best bit was when he put it under the cold tap and the rod snapped. Everyone laughed, but it was supposed to happen like that.

At the table next to Barney's, Luke Bailey swung back on two legs of his chair and just at the critical moment, Jamal gave him a little shove and he crashed to the floor. The class went silent. Mr Lawson stared, long and hard, while Luke, oblivious to the teacher, slowly got himself back up and gave a bow to the rest of the class.

"Out! Get out! Now!"

Luke slouched his way out into the corridor.

They saw him once, peeping in through the window in the classroom door and making a silly face. Carly pointed and called out, "Look, Sir!"

"Silence! Or the whole class will come back here at break."

Barney pretended he'd forgotten about seeing him at the end of the lesson.

Drama next.

Barney liked the drama room. It was soundproofed, and painted black, and very warm. The teacher smiled a lot and said encouraging things, and they didn't have to write anything down. They acted out little scenes in small groups, and he was put with Harriet and Jody and Moses and it was all right.

At break time, Barney sat outside on the bench. A crowd of girls from his class went past and one of them said hello quite nicely, but the others laughed and Barney wondered whether it had been a dare or something. He ate his chocolate bar out of his lunch box. Jamal and Pete came past. They didn't notice him.

Last lesson of the morning was PE. They got changed, then they were split into two groups.

Mr Malik took their group out onto the field. "Okay, boys. Cross-country running. Timed trials, round the track. Warm up first."

Max and Carl groaned. Jamal started to complain about his ankle. But Barney's spirits soared. At last! Something he could do.

His head was free; he felt the air rush past, his feet found their own rhythm. He knew when to go fast, how to pace it, how to keep his breathing regular and steady. Soon he was way out in the lead. His heart beat fast and his feet danced along

the grass; his whole body seemed to wake up.
Three laps, four. A final sprint to
the finishing line.

"Well done, lad." Mr
Malik clicked the
stopwatch. "After school,
Wednesday next week.
Under twelves. Okay?
You're a definite."

The next boy to come in
was Joe. When he'd got his
breath back, and finished his
leg stretches, he came over to
stand near Barney. "Cool. You're fast!"

Barney shrugged. "Thanks."

Carl, Pete and Jamal gave Barney and Joe a
hard time back in the changing rooms. They
kicked their stuff around the dusty floor and
played catch with Barney's trainers. But Barney
didn't care. The thrill of being first stayed with
him all afternoon.

On the bus home he hardly heard David Blake's
sarcastic comments until another voice piped up.
"Who do they think they are? Calling you that.
I'd thump them one if it was me."

Barney looked up.

"You should thump them," Carly repeated.

"What are you doing here?" Barney blurted out.

"Going to my nan's. On Greenhill estate. So?"

Just his luck.

They'd almost got to Barney's stop. He watched Carly stand up, ring the bell and swing off, her tatty bag spilling out bits of paper onto the pavement. He stayed on the bus for the next stop, wherever that was. It seemed a long way. Still, it was better than getting off with Carly. She was like a leech, the way she latched onto people, even though it was obvious they didn't want to be friends. That was all he needed!

He'd never been this far along the main road before. He decided to walk back along the river. It wasn't as easy as he thought. There wasn't a proper path, and he had to fight his way through a thicket of prickly trees and then a patch of bog, and his shoes got caked in mud. He was starving.

He stopped when he reached the weir. It was amazing, the way the water spilled over the concrete edge and foamed and curled underneath. He'd seen a programme, once, about a canoeist drowning at a weir like that, sucked under, trapped by the undertow.

Nearly home. In the bottom field a small boy rode round on a battered old BMX bike. He

watched Barney, then started showing off, riding too fast, and fell off. Barney smiled. He turned up the first road of the estate.

"Hiya Barney!"

Carly's voice rang out from the open window of the end house on Sycamore Terrace.

"Wanta see our kittens? Nan's cat's got three cutey little kittens. Barneeey?"

Her voice echoed after him. Head down, Barney ran for it.

Chapter seven

Saturday morning. Barney felt like he'd got a huge smile stretched across his chest.

Nine o'clock. The house was quiet. Mum was working today, so she'd have left ages ago, and Dad must still be asleep. Barney pulled on combats, T-shirt, trainers. He felled the army of Orcs arranged on the bedroom windowsill with one hand as he pulled the curtains back with the other. Sunshine flooded in.

He switched the kettle on in the kitchen, poured himself a huge bowl of chocolate crispy puffs, which he ate standing up, then made a mug of tea for Dad. Two sugars. He took it upstairs.

"Tea, Dad. You're taking me to Mick's, remember? Ten o'clock."

Dad opened one eye and groaned. "It's Saturday morning, kid."

"If you bought me a bike, I could get there by

myself. And you could stay in bed longer."

"That's a fact," Dad said. "Good idea. We'll speak to your mother about it."

That would mean no. Too much traffic. Not safe. Too far. She'd have all the reasons.

"Why wait?" Barney said. "We could get one today. There's a bike shop by the station, right near Mick's house. End of season sale. Mountain bikes fifty quid off."

"How do you know that?"

"I don't. But they did last year."

"We're not made of money, Barney. Moving house costs a fair old whack."

"It would be compensation," Barney said. "Since I'm the one who's left all his friends behind. And I never had a choice, either."

Dad laughed. "Bribery and corruption! Taking unfair advantage of a forty-year-old who is only half awake."

"I even brought you tea," Barney said. "So?"

"So what?"

"So, shall we get me a bike?"

"Not today. We'll see how the money's going, end of the month. And talk to Mum. You could start saving up, though."

"How?"

"You want to get a paper round or something."

"You have to be thirteen," Barney said. "And there isn't a shop. Haven't you noticed? There isn't anything."

He slammed the door. Big mistake. He knew as soon as he'd done it. He needed that lift from Dad.

Barney went downstairs and opened the back door. The small garden looked bare and uninviting. He squelched over the mud and pulled himself up so he could look over the wooden fence. There was a jumble of weeds, a thin passageway between their fence and the one belonging to the house behind – big enough to

squeeze into. He scrambled over the fence, dropped down into the weedy gap, and then ran along it. He came out on the top edge of the field. Cool. He started running. He did three laps. The small kid with the bike stood and watched him.

Must be nearly ten. Barney squeezed himself back along the passageway and over the fence into the garden. Dad was in the kitchen, eating fried egg and sausage.

"Want some?" he asked with his mouth full.

Barney shook his head.

"I'll just finish this and then we'll go to your mate's."

"Thanks, Dad. Sorry, about earlier."

"I know. It hasn't been easy for you. But you'll get used to it."

* * * * *

Dad dropped Barney off at the end of Mick's road. He ran down the busy street, past the newsagent, past the fish and chip shop, the old-fashioned barber's, into the flats and up the stairs two at a time. He pressed the buzzer for Mick's.

"Who is this?" Mick's voice came, in a funny spy accent.

Barney laughed. "Let us in, then."

It was like going home. The flat smelled

comforting: a mix of dusty carpets, fried bacon, and damp washing.

"Hi, Barney! We've missed you!" Mick's mum tried to hug him but he managed to dodge out of the way and into Mick's bedroom just in time.

They shut the door and turned up the volume on the computer.

They had bacon sandwiches for lunch, and then Barney borrowed one of Mick's old skateboards and they went down the street to the park. Mick showed off his new skills. Barney was out of practice.

"What's it like, your new place?" Mick asked as they sat on the kerb for a breather.

"Okay. Too quiet. No shops. The river's cool, though."

Mick shook his head. "No shops! Imagine." He was quiet for a bit. Then he said, "What about your school?"

"What about it? It's just school. Too big."

"Ours, too. And there's all these kids acting crazy. Like, they don't know when to shut up. Don't want to learn anything. It's a pain."

Barney nodded. He felt a bit better, hearing Mick say that. He'd imagined that everything would be better at Mick's school. "What's Dan doing this weekend?" he asked.

"Visiting his grandad," Mick said.

Was that why Mick had called Barney? If Dan had been around, would he have bothered?

"Come on. Let's look in the bike shop window. I'm getting a new bike soon." Barney started walking towards the station, skateboard under one arm.

They each chose one they liked. Then they looked at the prices. "Some hope!" Mick said.

"If we had bikes, we could go off places by ourselves," Barney said.

Mick looked doubtful. "Have you got your new Playstation yet?"

Barney shook his head. "Nah. Not yet."

"What do you do all the time, then?"

"Go down the river, run, just hang out. You know."

Mick creased up his nose. "Boring."

It was, Barney supposed. Especially without anyone to hang out with.

They skated back via the model shop, the joke shop and the market with the cheap sweet stall. They each bought a bag of pic'n'mix, and Barney stocked up on sherbet lemons, which were still his favourite.

At five, Barney left Mick and walked to the precinct where Mum worked in the card shop. She was getting ready to leave.

"Had a good time?" Mum chattered on.

Barney stopped listening. Had he had a good time? Sort of, but inside he felt all churned up again. He felt at home in the town. He knew where to go, and there were people everywhere, things happening. Driving back to the new house, he felt suddenly sad and empty. It wouldn't be long, he thought, till Mick forgot all about him.

"What's up?" Mum asked.

"Nothing."

"Chicken curry for tea." She smiled. "And you can chose a video from the Bridge shop if you like. I can take it back on Monday on my way to work."

See, it was easy for her. She came into town by car to work, it wasn't much different. And she had all her projects for the new house and garden to keep her happy. She liked the quiet.

At the video shop, Barney chose the new James Bond. Dad and he watched it after supper while Mum sat at the kitchen table, planning the new garden.

"Did you talk to Mum about the bike?" Barney asked Dad, just before he went to bed.

"Not yet. Wait a bit, eh? When I've made a bit more on the lorry. I've got a long trip coming up next month, to Eastern Europe. After that, maybe?"

Barney sighed. That was ages away. Mick would have forgotten him completely by then.

"I need a new skateboard, too."

"What's happened to the old one?"

"Wheel's broken. It's rubbish."

"I'll take a look tomorrow, see if we can fix it. Now, bed! Go!"

Chapter Eight

Dad didn't have time to look at the skateboard in the morning. He'd arranged to meet up with some mates, to go and look at a car. Barney moped about the house for a bit, until Mum got fed up with him.

"Have you done your homework?"

"Mum! It's the weekend."

"Well, have you? Bring me that planner book and show me."

Barney dragged it out of the school bag. The cover ripped slightly. He showed her the page.

"Maths. French. Art. See? You haven't done any of them. So get on with it now, Barney."

Barney kicked the bag.

He pulled out the art book. "Draw a landscape," the teacher had said.

"Where do you think you're going?" Mum shouted.

"Out. It's for Art." Barney slammed the back door behind him.

It was cold, sitting still. He sketched the river. It looked a mess. He added a moorhen, but that went wrong too. When he tried to rub it out, it made a smudge. He pulled out the whole page and crumpled it up and threw it into the water. He started again. It was too hard. There was too much to put in. Once you started looking, you saw more and more.

Barney shivered. He looked round, quickly, as if someone was watching him. Nobody there. He drew another line, shaded in some water. Too boring, he thought. He added a small figure, arms up in the river, like the 'NO SWIMMING' sign.

Behind him, something made a noise. He swung round. The boy on the BMX was racing off in the other direction. Barney rolled up his art book and shoved it into his pocket. He was freezing. Once he'd got back to the field he started to run. He should be practising, really, for the cross-country trials. He did three laps of the field, till he was properly out of breath. He felt better after that. No sign of the boy. He went home.

"Isn't Dad back?"

"He's probably gone down the pub with his mates," Mum said, spooning sauce onto Barney's pasta.

"He said he'd mend my skateboard."

"Shall I help? After lunch?"

They surveyed the cracked board together. "It's not safe like that," Mum said. "Even with the wheels fixed. You need a new one. For Christmas, maybe."

That was three months away. How would he ever catch up with Mick now?

"Want to come down the garden centre with me, Barney?" Mum asked.

He shook his head.

"You okay by yourself, then? Dad won't be long."

He watched her drive off. The empty afternoon stretched ahead of him. He watched telly for a bit. Then he was so bored he lined up all the Dwarves and Orcs on his bedroom floor and staged a mock battle. He wondered whether you could die of boredom.

A white car drew up at the end of the road. Dad got out. Barney ran down the stairs to meet him. Dad was holding something behind his back. For a wild moment, Barney thought it might be a new skateboard.

"Secondhand down the car boot sale," Dad grinned. He held out a large terracotta plant pot. "Mum'll love it."

Barney wondered what it would sound like smashing into a million pieces.

He scowled at Dad. "There's nothing to do here," he said. "Nothing."

"You need some mates," Dad said. "Can't you ring someone, get them over?"

"Like who?" Barney touched the plant pot with his toe. One kick and it would crash over on the path.

Dad held out his hands. "I don't know, do I? Someone from your new class? Mick? Dan? I'll take a look at that skateboard if you want."

"No point. It's wrecked."

Barney went back into the house and slumped in front of the television. He watched the athletics, then a stupid quiz show.

Finally, he went out into the street with the broken skateboard. It wouldn't run smoothly, kept jerking to one side. He tried it on the lower road, which had more of a slope. The BMX boy was watching from his front garden.

Barney stopped. "Hello," he said.

The boy didn't answer.

"I saw you," Barney said, "this morning. Spying."

The boy looked embarrassed. "Wasn't," he said.

"Nice bike," Barney said, even though it was an old wreck. "I'm getting a bike."

"What sort?"

"Mountain bike, probably," Barney said.

"What, new?"

"Yes. What's your name?"

"Lee."

"Hi, Lee. Barney. See ya around." Barney skated down to the field. He sat on the tree stump at the far end. After a bit, he heard Lee on his bike. Lee stood to one side, waiting for something to happen.

"Aren't there any other kids?" Barney said.

"Only little ones. And some girls, along Cedar Close, but they don't play out."

Barney nodded. Lee moved a bit closer. "Lots of houses are still for sale. They've only just finished them. So there might be more, soon. Like you. How old are you?"

"Eleven. Nearly twelve," Barney said. "You?"

"Nine."

He looked much younger. Small, and scraggy. Bit like Carly.

"Got to go. See you!" Barney said.

"Want to play, tomorrow?" Lee called after him. Barney didn't answer.

Chapter Nine

Monday.

"Hello, Barn Owl. Want a ciggie?" David Blake flashed a packet in front of Barney and then pretended to stumble and fall on Barney as the bus pulled out into traffic. Barney tried to ignore him. He was also trying to ignore Carly, in the seat behind him on the bus. She kept touching his shoulder and whispering things. Except she didn't know how to whisper. She might as well have shouted to the entire bus crowd.

Barney cringed. It was like that all the way to school. On the way to register he suddenly remembered he'd left his art book at home, and he hadn't done his French or maths homework. His stomach started to hurt again.

At registration, Mr Parnell handed him a note:

Lunchtime detention: room M11. Mr Lawson (Science)

Oh no.

French wasn't too bad. They had to pretend they were buying things in a shop. The teacher took their books in at the end of the lesson. Barney didn't say anything about the homework he hadn't done. Their usual teacher was away for maths, so that was okay. Then it was break. Barney went outside and stood on the edge of the field.

The bell went. Barney scurried along the corridor, trying to remember the way to the Year Seven lockers to get his PE kit.

"Barney! You're going the wrong way! It's PE next." Moses, from his tutor group, pointed up the corridor.

"I've got to get my stuff," Barney shouted above the din. It was like running uphill, or swimming against the current. He finally pushed his way through to the lockers and fumbled for his keys.

Where were they?

They should have been tied to his wallet. But his wallet wasn't there. When had he last had it? On the bus. He thought about David Blake. Perhaps he'd stolen it? Barney checked his other pocket, and then his bag. No luck.

The corridor was quiet, now. Everyone in their

classrooms, starting the next lesson. What should he do? If he went to PE without his kit he'd be in worse trouble. He was already late.

"Bunking off lessons, are we?" Two Year Nine girls giggled at him. "Naughty!"

He recognised them: the girls on the bus who knew David Blake.

"I've lost my key," Barney spluttered.

"Ahh! Poor you." They leaned against the lockers, menacing.

Footsteps clicked along the corridor. Relieved, Barney looked up to see the Head of Year Seven advancing. She spoke sharply to the girls.

"What's going on here? You should be in lessons. Get moving. Quick. See me at lunchtime, Jessica Adams and Michaela Wade." She turned to Barney. "What are you doing here?"

Barney's eyes were watering. He blinked hard. "I've lost my key. And they were on my wallet, and I've lost that too and it's got my bus pass in and so I can't get home and I'm late now ..." The words came tumbling out.

She pulled a set of keys from her pocket. "Locker master key. There. Which one's yours? Now, get what you need and hurry to class. What's your name?"

"Barney Eliot."

She smiled. "Sounds familiar. Mr Parnell's group, yes?"

He nodded.

"Where should you be?"

"PE."

"Know the way?"

"Yes."

"Run along then. Tell your tutor about your wallet this afternoon. Yes? He'll help you sort it out."

Everyone was already changed, jumping up and down in the gym. Barney got his kit on and sidled in, unnoticed. He went to stand near Joe. They did wall bars and ropes, and then they each had a go on the trampoline.

"Lunch?" Joe asked at the end of the lesson.

Barney shook his head miserably. "Got detention."

He wasn't the only one in M11. About ten of them had to write what they'd done wrong, and then do a worksheet about behaviour. Barney wrote a long explanation of how it wasn't his fault. He didn't know how to spell *fault*. And he wished he could remember the little kid's name. He wrote about what the kid had done to his ears. It took longer than half an hour. He couldn't find Joe afterwards, so he ate his dinner by himself.

He forgot about his wallet and key until the end of registration, and then Mr Parnell was too busy and the bell went for the afternoon lesson.

History.

Adam! That was his name. Of course. The kid who did that thing to his ears. Barney watched him sticking a blob of bubble gum in the back of some poor girl's hair.

It wasn't the usual history teacher, who was off sick. This one, a new supply teacher, insisted that they sit boy/girl all round the room, and Barney, of course, had ended up next to Carly.

Now they were supposed to copy down lots of writing from the overhead projector for their Ice Man project. The writing was too small. Barney started getting a headache. He looked at the clock. Two thirty. What was he going to do about his missing wallet? Bet that David Blake had nicked it. His bus pass cost nearly thirty pounds. He had to get it back. How did you get a new locker key? That cost money too.

Carly nudged him in his side.

"Ouch. Don't do that!" Barney hissed.

"She's talking to you, idiot."

The teacher was moving slowly between the desks. She stopped beside Carly and Barney, and picked up Barney's exercise book.

"Well?" she said, peering at him.

"Sorry?" Barney said.

"Have you?"

"Have I?" Barney echoed.

"Finished? No. You've hardly started. And what you have done is riddled with mistakes. It's virtually illegible. A total mess. All you had to do was copy. But no. That's too hard for you. You've got better things to do, like chat, and fidget, and stare out of the window."

As her voice became louder and more sarcastic Barney felt himself begin to shake. His stomach did a sort of loop the loop, his legs began to tremble and his eyes suddenly saw everything in red. He put his hands over his ears to shut her out.

The teacher angrily grabbed his arm.

That was it.

"Stop it!" he shouted. He shoved her away, stood up, pushed his chair over and rushed for the door.

He wrenched it open and ran down the corridor, the blood pounding in his ears. The teacher's voice echoed in his head, cruel and nagging and unbearable.

Someone called out his name. He rushed on, towards the exit door at the end of the corridor and out across the field, just like he'd imagined it that very first day, on and on, through the school gates and down the road.

His breath rasped at first, caught up in a sort of sobbing noise he couldn't stop, but then as his feet found their own rhythm, the strong steady beat of his

heart settled into a pattern he knew: the measured pace of the long-distance runner. And as he ran, he started to realise exactly what he'd done.

He'd shouted back at a teacher.

He'd run out of school.

But he didn't feel sick, or frightened, any more; he felt strong. As if he'd done something incredibly brave and powerful.

Because it wasn't right, what they did. How they treated him. Not David Blake or Mr Lawson or those Year Nine girls or Adam or that mean, nasty, sarcastic supply teacher. Why should he put up with it?

As he reached the big bend in the main road, he started to slow down. What now?

Chapter Ten

No one would be at home. Dad had left early that morning for his next long trip. Mum would be at the card shop. Without his wallet, he had no key. No key, so he couldn't get in, and no money. He'd have to walk it. He wasn't completely sure of the way. He kept on running, although more slowly and steadily, along the next section of the main road. Past the pub, past the row of shops and then the beginning of a big estate where Moses and Joe lived. Barney wished he'd moved here, instead of Greenhill. He'd have got to know lots of people by now.

He ran on, past a primary school, and blocks of flats and a church. This was where the bus turned off. Barney went down the steep hill. Then there was a horrible long stretch of dual carriageway with no path. He kept to the grass verge; the wet soaked through his school shoes and his feet began to feel sore. It was miles. Much further than it seemed on the bus. Barney began to feel scared.

A car slowed down and a man wound down his window. "Want a lift?"

"No thanks." Barney looked round for somewhere to run to if the man started getting funny. Never accept lifts from strangers. He'd been told often enough. And there were some strange people around. You saw it on the news: men kidnapping children.

The car drove off again. Barney jogged on. He was getting a stitch. A lorry whooshed past so close Barney felt his hair lift in the draught. It honked its horn. He thought of Dad, driving down through France, and Germany, and into Eastern Europe. Barney wished he were with Dad now, driving with the radio on, planning where to spend the night. One day, that's what he'd do – go on a really long journey. Canada. Wild, snowy mountains and woods and lakes. Or maybe the Himalayas … or somewhere hot, like the Sahara Desert. Or an amazing city with trams and parks and loads of shops selling cool stuff, but near the sea – surfing beaches, coral reefs …

The dual carriageway ended at the roundabout. It took him ages to cross, but it was a relief to be back on smaller roads. He was pretty sure he was going the right way now. It must be after the end of school. Any minute now, the bus would go past and David Blake and those girls would see him walking home. He decided to cut across, away from the road, into the woodland that skirted the road. In any case, it had begun to rain. It would be drier under the trees.

It was dark, too, under the dense canopy of leaves and creepers. Roots jutted out of the ground so that Barney had to concentrate hard not to trip. The rain made a rustling sound on the leaves; he kept looking round to check no one was following him. It seemed to be taking a long time to get anywhere.

He tried to imagine the scene at school after he'd run out: shocked silence, perhaps, at first. Then someone giggling, the teacher getting angry. Would she have gone and reported what had happened? Would someone telephone his mum at work?

He hurried on, stumbling over the long ropes of

creeper that dangled through overhanging ivy, brushing through low-hanging branches. Eventually he trudged back to the road. That would be easier.

His feet ached; they were soaked. And he was so tired and cold and hungry. He was still a long way from home. He'd be in terrible trouble.

At last the road broadened out. There were street lights, and the first new houses, and things began to look familiar. Finally he reached the lane down to the Greenhill estate. Mum's car was in the drive.

Barney knocked on the front door. It opened almost immediately.

"Barney! You're so late! I was worried! What happened?"

One look at her face and Barney knew she hadn't heard anything from school.

"I lost my wallet," he said. "With my bus pass and money and everything, so I had to walk all the way home."

"What – oh, Barney, why on earth didn't you ask someone to lend you some money? It's miles! You silly thing – look at you! You're soaked. Where's your coat?"

He tried to explain about leaving it in his locker and the lost key, and it all sounded quite believable. Mum fussed over him and made him have a bath and then hot soup and he ate a huge supper and didn't mind going to bed early for once.

He heard the phone ring: Dad. Mum's voice drifted upstairs. "He was drenched. Exhausted. I know ... day off tomorrow. Yes, I'll take the day off work. Poor Barney. And you? Good. Take care, love."

Sorted. He didn't have to think about school the next day. A big smile spread across his face. He went to sleep almost immediately.

Chapter Eleven

He woke up twice in the night, sweating and thirsty and with a terrible sore throat.

When he woke properly in the morning it was after nine. His head hurt, his legs ached, he felt awful. No school, but no fun either. He was ill for real!

The next few days passed in a daze. He had a high temperature. Flu, Mum thought.

"That walk home in the rain was the last straw," she said.

She took the whole week off work so she could be there to look after him.

By Thursday he was feeling better, but he might as well have the week off, Mum said. No point getting run down at this stage of the term. He watched videos, and she read to him, like she used to when he was little and when she wasn't working full time. She dug out a book she'd had as a child from one of the boxes still in the garage.

"The boy's got the same name as you, Barney," she told him. "And they've made it into a film now. *Stig of the Dump*." It made him feel cosy and safe, being read to. His eyes hurt too much to read by himself.

At the weekend, she phoned Mick's mum and invited her to come over with Mick.

Mick couldn't come. "Going to some paintballing party," Mum said, "whatever that is."

It was raining, anyway. Barney spent most of the time indoors. He downloaded some new games on the old computer, but it was so slow that he got fed up with it.

"School tomorrow," Mum said on Sunday night. "I've got to go into work. And you're better enough. Bored stiff with being at home, I bet."

His stomach started to twist and knot.

"I've got you a new wallet and a bus pass," Mum went on. "I'll give you some money for a new locker key."

It made everything worse, somehow, her being so nice. He couldn't tell her what school was really like. What he'd done.

* * * * *

"I've cooked you an egg," Mum said as Barney came downstairs in his school uniform. "And I'll give you a lift today, since it's your first day back and I expect you're a bit nervous."

Barney didn't think he could manage an egg. His stomach felt full already.

Mum dropped him off in the school car park and Barney watched her drive away.

"Hi, Barney! Are you better now?" Moses came up the drive with Joe.

"You missed the cross-country trials," Joe said. "But I expect they'll let you in. You were easily the best."

The three of them walked into school together. Joe said he'd come to Reception to help Barney get a new locker key.

Afterwards, they went to the tutor room for the register. Barney handed his tutor the note Mum had written. Mr Parnell read it and smiled.

"Better now? Good. We'll have a little chat

at lunchtime. Don't look so worried! Just to fill you in on what you've missed."

First lesson was drama.

They played 'killer wink' as the warm-up. That got everyone in a good mood. Jamal managed to kill the whole group before anyone guessed. Luke took about five noisy minutes to die. Carly fell down so fast she bumped her head and had to sit out for the next exercise, which was pretending to be a chair. Barney was an electric chair, and everyone laughed at the voice he did for it. It had an American accent.

"Now we're going on with last week's scenes, exploring feelings about bullying," Miss Almond said. "Get into your small groups."

Barney looked around. He'd missed the last lesson, so he didn't have a group.

Miss Almond noticed him. "Who would you like to join, Barney?"

He shrugged. "Dunno. Joe and Moses?"

"Carly's group is smaller than the others," Miss Almond said.

He frowned.

Miss Almond bent down, so she could speak more privately. "She needs a hand, especially with this subject. No one wants to go with her. Would you mind, Barney? Please? To help me out?"

What could he say?

In the end, they acted out a scene on a bus; Barney just thought about what it was like with David Blake. It was very realistic, and even Carly was good. Everyone clapped and said theirs was the best. Miss Almond beamed.

"Thank you, and well done everybody. Merits for everyone, and an extra merit for Carly, Barney and Jody." She went round the circle, stamping everyone's merit pages in their planners with her special drama frog stamp. When she got to Barney, she spoke very quietly.

"Such good acting, Barney, it almost seemed as if the bullying was real."

Back in the centre of the room she clapped her hands for silence.

"What would we do if we were being bullied or knew someone who was? Don't call out. Hands up."

"You should tell someone. Your mum or a teacher or someone."

"That's right, Harriet. We have a special policy about it in this school. But we can't help you if we don't know. So please, always, tell someone."

The bell went for the next lesson.

* * * * *

Barney had dinner with Moses and Joe, and afterwards they went out onto the field, but it was raining so hard they ended up in the library instead. They looked at comics together.

"Oh no! What's the time? I'm supposed to meet Mr Parnell at one thirty!" Barney raced off down to the staffroom.

"How's it going, today?" Mr Parnell asked.

"Okay," Barney mumbled.

"Your drama teacher is very pleased with you, I hear."

Barney shifted onto the other foot.

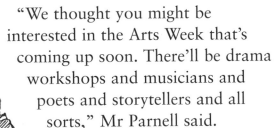

"We thought you might be interested in the Arts Week that's coming up soon. There'll be drama workshops and musicians and poets and storytellers and all sorts," Mr Parnell said.

Barney looked at his feet.

"A chance to meet different people, make new friends, maybe. Now, something else we need to chat about."

Barney's neck went hot.

"Catching up last week. Best if you look through a friend's books, copy the notes. And speak to each teacher, to explain. Okay?"

Barney nodded.

"But don't worry too much. Don't want to get ill again, do you?" Mr Parnell peered more closely at Barney. "How's the travelling going? You have to get a bus, don't you?"

"Yes. It's okay."

"And the lost wallet. Did you go to Lost Property? Miss Farley can help you there."

Barney nodded again. He was still waiting for what Mr Parnell was going to say about the history lesson.

Nothing, apparently.

The bell went.

"Run along then."

Barney let out a huge sigh of relief.

* * * * *

At the end of school, Barney walked along the road with Moses and Joe.

"Want to come back to ours?" Moses asked.

"I have to get home, today," Barney said. "But another time, yes."

"Cool."

David Blake didn't get on the bus. Mum had got home early. Fish and chips for tea. Dad phoned from somewhere in France. Not such a bad day after all.

Chapter Twelve

The rest of the week made up for it. One not bad day in exchange for four terrible ones. Mr Lawson picked on him in science, Adam did that thing with his ears in the middle of music, and when Barney yelled out he got into trouble and had to do a lunchtime detention. The English teacher moaned about his spelling and handwriting. He forgot to bring in the history homework on the right day. He hadn't done it, anyway. It was the project on the Ice Man.

"Why haven't you done it?" Mum asked on Thursday evening when he was trying to explain why he'd got to stay late at school to finish it on Friday. "You've just got to get organised, Barney. You have to take responsibility for yourself now."

"It's too hard," Barney said. "I don't have enough notes. I missed the work."

"Let me phone school and explain. It's not your fault you were ill," she said.

Barney didn't want her to phone. "It's okay," he said. "I'll do it after school. Be home late."

"Well, I'm not home till after six on Fridays anyway," Mum said. "I'll get pizzas on the way back to cheer us both up."

* * * * *

Barney sat in the dusty classroom, his history book in front of him. There were bits of information about the Ice Man from different sources, like newspapers, or science reports. You had to look at the sources, and say what they proved. The Ice Man was found in some mountains on the Italian-Austrian border. He was more than six thousand years old. He'd been preserved in a glacier. He had a flint knife and an axe and a bow and arrow with him. They found berries in his stomach.

Barney felt sleepy. He started to think what the Ice Man might look like. He imagined him something like Stig, in the story Mum had read him. Shaggy black hair, grunting, making a fire by rubbing sticks. Sharpening flint stones to a knife-edge.

Barney's eyes began to close.

He was with Stig, or the Ice Man, or whoever,

down by the river. The roaring sound from the weir was getting louder and louder. They were standing on the weir, fishing with a sharpened flint on the end of a long stick, and then ...

"Barney? It's time to pack up. Put the book on my desk as you go out."

Everyone else was already leaving.

Barney still hadn't finished the work. But it was too late now. He waited for a bus.

No one else got on from the school stop. It seemed darker than usual. The wind blew litter and fallen leaves along the kerb. The rain had stopped. Instead of going straight home, Barney went down to the river.

Pity there wasn't an old quarry like Stig lived in. There wasn't really anywhere you could make a den like that. One or two big trees, though – good for a tree house. Mick and he could make one. When Mick came over ... if he ever did.

Barney suddenly noticed Lee's old BMX, leaned against the wire netting that ran along one edge of the field. Where was Lee? Watching him from somewhere, as usual? Barney looked round, listened. Nothing.

Well, not exactly nothing. If you listened, the air was full of noises – rustlings of undergrowth, the scrape of branches against each other, birdcalls, insects, the hum of the overhead electric cable.

And under and over it all, the roar of the weir.

Barney left his school bag on the grass and edged along the muddy riverbank towards the roaring sound. The river was almost up to the top of the banks, swollen from the weeks of rain. It bubbled and boiled, a brown, muddy, swirling current in the middle, whirling branches and debris downstream.

Barney went round the bend in the river and then stopped, mouth open. On the lip of the weir, edging his way across, was Lee. He had his back to Barney. In one hand he held a stick which he was using to balance himself, all the while concentrating on the concrete edge, resisting the flow that wanted to sweep him over and drag him down. What did he think he was doing? Couldn't he see how dangerous it was?

"Lee!" Barney shouted, but his voice got drowned in the roar of the water. He tried again. "Oi! Lee! Get back here!"

Barney scrambled along the bank. As he reached the weir Barney saw Lee hesitate and turn round slightly, as if he'd heard something. In that moment he lost concentration. His foot slipped. Barney watched in horror as Lee tumbled over the edge.

Chapter Thirteen

Lee gave a shout, which got swallowed up by the sound of the water, and then he seemed to disappear, pulled under by the swirling current.

"Help! Someone help!" Barney croaked out.

Lee bobbed back up to the surface, gasping and gulping for air, arms thrashing wildly. Barney grabbed the end of a long branch embedded in a jumble of nettles, wrenched it free and tried to manoeuvre it out over the river to reach Lee. His feet kept slipping on the mud. The log was too heavy. He tried again, splashing the log down as near to Lee as he could.

Barney shouted out again. "Lee! Grab the log."

Lee's wet head surfaced. His eyes looked terrible. Empty, dark, afraid. His arms thrashed feebly out towards the log. The current was pulling him further away from the bank. His head went under again.

It was no use. The log was too heavy. Lee was already exhausted, freezing cold. The way the weir was shaped meant a roll of water spun continually in the middle of the river. You had to break free of it to have any chance of surviving. Barney pushed the log further out, but it meant he had less leverage, and he was in danger of slipping into the river himself if Lee did manage to grab hold of it. He looked round frantically, calling for help.

And there was someone. He heard the thud of footsteps and a girl's voice calling out, and round the bend of the river came Carly.

"What's happened?" she called out as she ran towards him. "What is it?"

"Lee. Fallen in. Grab the end of this." Barney seized the chance to push the log a little further out, just as Lee bobbed up again. "Now!" he yelled.

"It's okay, Lee. We'll get you out!" Carly shouted too. "Hold the end and we'll pull."

"He's too weak," Barney said. "He's exhausted. His hands are blue with cold. You'll have to get someone. Run back to the houses."

"There isn't time," Carly said. "We just have to get him out. He'll drown if we don't."

Barney didn't argue. She was right. "One more go, then."

Together they steered the log into a better position. Lee's hand flailed round, touched the small branch at one end. The feel of it seemed to give him energy. With huge effort, he heaved himself nearer and then caught hold of the branch with both hands. The sudden increase in weight took Barney by surprise. He staggered, slipped, lost his grip and for one terrible moment thought they'd lost Lee back into the river. But he was holding on for life. For real.

Carly squealed, but she braced her feet, pulled back and held onto the log just enough to stop it spinning off into the river with Lee still clinging to the end branch. Barney grabbed on again.

"Heave!" Carly yelled. "Pull towards you."

How could it be so heavy? They heaved and dragged at the sodden wood, and bit by bit they drew Lee closer to the bank, out of the spinning vortex of the weir.

His lips were blue, his eyes shut. Perhaps they were too late?

"The branch is going to break off," Carly suddenly yelled. "Lee, grab hold of the trunk. Not the branch."

Lee didn't move.

"Get ready," Carly told Barney. "Get a grip on him as soon as he's close."

Barney leaned out over the river, waiting for the sodden mass, terrified that it was a corpse they were hauling out of the water. He grabbed Lee's leg, then the belt in his jeans, and pulled with all his strength.

Barney's ears were full of the roar of the water, his nose filled with the stench of river mud. His hands were numb with cold. But he kept hold. It was easier now; the body bobbed and floated in the calmer water near the bank. And then Lee lifted his head, his whole body shuddered, and he began to choke and splutter. He was alive.

Together, Carly and Barney pulled him up over the edge of the bank and rolled him onto the path. He began to vomit water and mud, and to shake violently. Barney pulled his own coat off and put it over the boy.

"Now run," Carly said. "Faster than you've ever run before. Get my nan. Someone. An ambulance. I'll stay with him."

Barney ran.

Chapter Fourteen

He ran all along the river path and across the field, and then cut through the passageway to the back garden without stopping. He scrambled over the wooden fence and hammered on the back door. Silence. He ran round to the front. No car. Of course, it was Friday: late night shopping at the precinct. There was no choice. Heart hammering, he ran on down The Beeches into Sycamore Terrace and knocked loudly on the front door of the end house.

A small dark woman opened the door and stared suspiciously at Barney.

"What do you want?"

"Sorry – help – there's a boy – the river – I'm Carly's friend Barney –" his words jumbled out.

"Calm down young man," she said. "Take it slow."

"Please," Barney said, "we need an ambulance.

This boy – Lee – fell in the river – he nearly
drowned –"

Carly's nan caught the panic. She dialled 999
with trembling hands, explained where the
ambulance should go, then grabbed a

blanket from the back of the sofa
in the front room and
struggled into her coat. She
still had her slippers on.

"We'll go by Lee's
house," she said, as they
hurried down the street
towards the river. "Not
that his mum'll be able to
do much. With the twin
babies and all. Poor
woman."

But nobody was in at Lee's
house. They hurried on, Carly's nan puffing and
wheezing. She stopped at the edge of the field and
thrust the blanket at Barney.

"You go on," she puffed.

Barney didn't want to, suddenly. He was afraid
of what he might find. Don't think about it, he
told himself. White skin, blue lips; what a dead
body looks like. Carly, all by herself. Run. Just
run!

He came round the bend in the river. Crouched on the bank, Carly was holding Lee's head and stroking his wet hair as if he were a kitten or something, and making reassuring noises.

Lee wasn't dead.

Carly smiled at Barney. "Thank goodness. Give us that blanket. Ambulance coming?"

Barney nodded. "And your nan."

By the time the ambulance crew arrived, they'd got Lee wrapped in the blanket and sitting up, still shivering all over. The ambulance crew said they'd have to take him into hospital; get him checked over. Then the police arrived, and wanted to ask lots of questions, and Barney and Carly had to explain the whole story over again.

"You should get a medal," Nan said. "You were both very brave indeed. Weren't they, officer?"

The policewoman tutted and went on about the dangers of children playing unsupervised near rivers and looked at Nan as if it was her fault. She didn't seem to understand that it was Carly's nan, not Lee's. She went back to her police car to wait for Lee's mum to return. Carly wanted to go in the ambulance with Lee, but Nan said no, they'd had enough excitement for one day, and in any case, she only had her slippers on, and they were coated with mud now. She invited Barney back too.

It seemed a good idea, really. Mum still wasn't back, and he was freezing. He picked up his school bag on the way back along the river, and his wet coat, and walked back alongside Carly.

He looked at her, sideways on. She wasn't so bad – not really. Not when you got to know her a bit. And she'd been really strong and practical with getting Lee out. So what if she couldn't write properly or didn't have the right sort of clothes or haircut? Those things wouldn't have helped, down by the river.

They had toast and hot chocolate, and told the story of what had happened one more time. They'd saved Lee's life, Nan said; she was sure of it.

After tea, Carly showed Barney the cat with her three grey kittens in the cardboard box in the corner of Nan's bedroom.

"They'll be needing homes," she said, "in two weeks' time. If you know anyone who wants one."

She looked wistfully at the kittens. "Though I don't see why Nan can't keep them all. Imagine, all by themselves, in a new home."

"They'll get used to it," Barney said. "They'll make new friends."

Chapter Fifteen

Lee's mum came round on Saturday to see Barney.

"I brought you this, Barney. It's not much, but it's to say thank you." She laid two twenty-pound notes on the table.

"It's too much," Mum started saying, but Barney was already thanking her. "I'm saving for a bike," he said.

Mum looked at him. "Are you?" she said. "I didn't know."

She drove him into town later. "I don't want you playing by the river when it's flooded and so dangerous," she said. "Lee's lucky to be alive."

He mooched about the centre while she was shopping at the supermarket. There wasn't anyone he knew in the park. There were some kids he knew from his old class kicking a can around the precinct, but he didn't stop to speak to them.

Things have moved on, he thought. We're all a bit different already.

Mum was waiting for him at the multi-storey car park, a newspaper tucked under one arm.

"It's got you in it!" she said. "Look!"

Barney peered at the tiny article on the second page. There wasn't even a photo. It mentioned Carly, though. He wondered what the kids at school would think.

He'd find out on Monday.

* * * * *

It started on the bus. Carly sat next to him; he couldn't really stop her.

David Blake did a wolf whistle when he saw them. "Got a girlfriend, Barnacle?"

Barney's neck went red.

"Something the cat dragged in?" David Blake went on.

"Do us a favour," Carly retorted. "Grow up!"

The two girls behind David Blake giggled loudly.

"He's all mouth," Carly said. "Like most bullies. Inside, he's scared."

Barney looked out of the window. He recognised the line of trees where he'd walked home that day. Gradually, things were becoming more familiar.

"I'll be friends out of school," Barney blurted out to Carly as they got off the bus. "Not in."

"Scaredy cat!" she said.

He waited for Moses and Joe to arrive.

There was a special assembly first thing instead of maths. Barney had forgotten about the Arts Week. Miss Almond explained about all the activities that would be taking place over the next week. Normal timetables were suspended. You could choose which workshops you went to instead. At the end of the week there would be a performance for parents and friends.

* * * * *

It was easier than Barney expected. As soon as the poet bloke said handwriting was all a question of taste, and not to worry about the spelling for now, it would all get sorted in good time, Barney started to relax.

The poet got them to listen to the sounds that words make, the patterns in sounds, the way sounds echo each other. They talked about soft sounds and hard sounds; they made sounds for water and sounds for skateboards. They listened to the sounds of blacksmiths beating iron on an anvil in a poem written hundreds of years ago. They listened to the sounds of silence, the gaps between the words. Words began to tap inside Barney's skull, asking to be let out. Barney began to write.

Once he'd started, he couldn't stop.

"We've opened the floodgate," the poet said, staring out of the window at the sky. Staring out of the window was also something to do with writing poems. You had to open your eyes and open your ears, and touch and smell and taste. They wrote poems about eating chocolate and chewing gum, about slices of melon, and the poet ("call me Finn") brought them the real things to eat first.

"Tap tap," the words went in Barney's head. "Let us out."

Finn showed them how to put the words in patterns on the page. They drew them in shapes. They made lines long or short, or let the lines walk over the edges, saying what they wanted to say.

"Listen," Finn said, "to how the words sound when you put them side by side. Then move them around. It's a game. Play with the words."

On Tuesday he showed them how to write a

haiku, with just three lines. You had to count the syllables – five, seven, five. On Wednesday they wrote sonnets, and on Thursday they came face to face with a villanelle.

"You can do it!" he told them.

The words danced and sang along the page, and it felt, Barney thought, a bit like running. Once your feet found the pattern. The more you did it, the easier it got. You warmed up first, did exercises before the long cross-country. Words could take you long distances too. Getting the words out changed the way you felt inside.

On Friday, Finn made them type up their poems on the computer. Barney's finger slowly tapped out the words. Finn helped him get the spellings right. They practised their performance all afternoon, ready for the evening show.

"You will come, won't you?" Barney had asked Mum, earlier in the week. Fridays were her working late days.

"Soon as I shut the shop," Mum said, "I'll be on my way. And Dad should be back earlier in the day, so he'll be there too."

Barney went back to Joe's house for tea after school on Friday. Moses came too. It seemed the obvious thing, really.

Their estate was older than Barney's. There

wasn't a field or a river. Barney told them about his field – perfect for training and football and bikes and everything. "You can come over at the weekend if you want."

* * * * *

The school hall had been done up; there were huge colourful flags hung round the walls (batik workshop), and red and gold tie-dyed cloths draped over tables (textiles workshop), and a wonderful display of huge paintings along the back wall (murals and graffiti workshop). Miss Almond had put candles on the tables, and small groups of chairs round them. The jazz club were already assembling. Barney was startled to see David Blake setting up the drum kit.

Barney settled himself next to Moses and Joe in the poetry performance group. They would be the last section, after contemporary dance.

Just before the lights were turned out, Barney craned round to check if his mum and dad had arrived yet. Yes.

Darkness. A hush rustled through the assembled audience. The first notes rang out from the saxophone.

At last it was their turn. Heart thudding, Barney followed the others up onto the stage.

Chapter sixteen

From the stage, the audience looked like a blur in
the darkness. It was easier that way. You couldn't
see individual faces. Barney waited. The words
tapped inside his head, rehearsing themselves.

His heart pounded, but he knew to trust
himself, like Finn said.

Aisha went first, with her poems about colour.
Then Joe, Moses and Barney did a football poem
and got everyone laughing. They bounced the
words like a ball between them, back and forth.
Michelle performed her love poem. Finally Barney
stepped forward to do his solo performance.

The hall went quiet. He started with the haiku.

Moving House
"So? You'll make new friends,"
they said. Alone in a crowd,
I wonder when, how?

The silence seemed to grow deeper. Everyone was paying attention. Barney went on to the next one. His voice got louder, more confident.

River
I go down the river after school.
It's cool. No one bothers me there.
Doesn't matter what I look like,
the style of my hair, the kind of shoes I wear.

No one bothers me.
No one shouts:
"Shut up! Say Sir!
You're a mess! Can't spell!"
"Get off our bus you creep! You smell!"

They make my life hell.

Down the river there's space,
No one in your face.
It's my special place.

Last poem. Barney took a deep breath.

We pulled a boy out of the water
all covered in weed and
stinking of river mud.

His face was corpse white.
I thought he was dead,
but we brought him back,

over the edge ...

Barney lost himself in his own words. They
kept on coming. His eyes were closed.

... seems like I'm always running,
moving on, running away,
but it's different this day:
this time I'm running to help someone else,
this time I'm running for friendship.

There was a moment's hush, and then everyone
started clapping and cheering and stamping their
feet. Barney felt his face go hot. Inside, he felt as
if the coiled eels in the pit of his belly had
unwound and swum off at last. He stepped back
into his place in the line of other kids on the
stage.

Finn leaned over the row, thumbs up. "Well done
everyone!"

Later, at home, Mum and Dad went on and on
about his brilliant performance.

"Standing up there! In front of all those people!

My son! Poetry! I'm so proud of you!" Dad gave
Barney a huge bear hug.

Mum sniffed back more tears. She'd cried all
through the poems. "To think what you've been
through. And not saying anything to us! That bus
journey! Those teachers! Moving house! Me making
you leave all your friends behind!"

"But in a way you were right, in the end," Barney
said, "about making new friends. I've got Joe and
Moses at school, now, and I've got Carly and Lee at
home, when I'm really desperate!" He laughed.

"And Mick and Dan," Dad said. "Once we've got
your bike sorted."

Barney grinned. "For real? A new bike?"

Dad nodded. "Didn't I promise? Soon as the next pay cheque comes in."

At bedtime, Barney looked at the calendar he'd hung by the window. The days he'd crossed off. Count down to the Christmas holidays. To the end of the school year. To the very last day of school ever.

"I think I'll survive after all," he told the Orc king wizard, still lying on his back on the windowsill with the rest of the army of Orcs.

Outside, the first owls began to hoot. Barney opened the window a little, to hear them better.

If he listened really carefully, he could just about

hear the sound of the water rushing over the weir. And the sky was full of stars, millions and millions of them, more than he'd ever seen from the flat.

"It's going to be okay," he said, out into the night.